Granny Squares

20 crochet projects with a vintage vibe

SUSAN PINNER

First published 2013 by
Guild of Master Craftsman Publications Ltd
Castle Place, 166 High Street, Lewes,
East Sussex BN7 1XU

Text © Susan Pinner, 2013
Copyright in the Work © GMC Publications Ltd, 2013

ISBN 978-1-86108-970-0

A catalogue record for this book is available from
the British Library.

Publisher Jonathan Bailey
Production Manager Jim Bulley
Managing Editor Gerrie Purcell
Senior Project Editor Virginia Brehaut
Copy Editor Judith Durant
Managing Art Editor Gilda Pacitti
Design Rebecca Mothersole
Photography Sian Irvine/Rebecca Mothersole

Set in Gibson
Colour origination by GMC Reprographics
Printed and bound in China

Contents

THE PROJECTS

GETTING STARTED

Introduction

Crochet is a technique for producing a handmade fabric (I'm almost sure there are no crochet machines) from yarn, thread, string or fabric strips. It is similar to knitting in that loops are pulled through loops, but crochet differs from knitting by using a single hook instead of two needles.

No one is quite sure when crochet first made an appearance, but we know today that the granny square was first published in *Weldon's Practical Needlework* in 1897 by The Weldon Company of London. It was referred to as a 'patchwork square' and described as a good way to use up leftover yarns.

The granny square can be made in a rainbow of colours or in one soft, subtle shade. And today's 'squares' aren't always square. These pick-up and put-down woolly wonders of handmade fabric come in all shapes and sizes, from stars to hexagons, circles and ripples. Sometimes referred to as motifs, many, many creative designs have appeared in the crochet world of the 21st century.

My first introduction to the granny square was way back in the early 1960s, when granny squares were the height of fashion and my best friend's granny tried teaching me to crochet. My first blanket followed a couple of years later and I have 'played hooky' many times since then.

I have never been so enthusiastic or passionate about this wonderfully addictive craft as I am today. Quick to work, fabulously affordable and portable too, this is one of the few crafts you can pop in your pocket or bag and take with you wherever you go. Crochet is a wonderfully creative hobby filled with fun and colour.

In the past few years, the humble granny square has appeared on catwalks from London to New York and has lost the stigma of being 'something your granny made'.

The granny square has come a long way from its origins and is as popular as ever, a true classic. This little gem can be varied in size and stitched together with others to make a fabulous heirloom blanket or a giant granny for cold nights. Appearing in many a sophisticated interiors magazine, crochet has become a popular creative craft.

When you have mastered the basics, I feel sure you will become as addicted to the hook as I am within a very short time. And, like me, you may choose to crochet at any available time and anywhere (always a good conversation starter in a public place). You can crochet with the family while watching TV. It is a calming, creative, feel-good craft, with a social side too – many a 'Knit and Natter' group includes crocheters and there are groups making granny-square blankets for charity. Crochet will keep your fingers supple and I'm told it can help stave off dementia too – all that counting is good for the brain.

With a little bit of patience, practice and this book, it will be easy, fun and affordable to get started with crochet. So buy a hook and a ball of yarn and learn the basic stitches, then begin to fill your home with colour and style.

Have fun and happy hooking!
Sue

CIRCULAR STOOL COVERS
page 56

TABLET COMPUTER CASE
page 60

STAR COASTERS
page 68

FELTED FLOWER BAG
page 72

STRING
SHOPPING BAG
page 76

GARDEN
SEAT COVER
page 80

HEXAGON DAISY BATH MAT
page 84

HEXAGON BED PILLOW
page 88
& *opposite* CAMPING BLANKET
page 92

HEXAGON BLANKET
page 96

FLOWER LIGHT SHADE
page 100

LACE LIGHT SHADE
page 104

LACE JAR COVER AND COASTERS
page 108

HEXAGON MINI CUSHION
page 112

DOUBLE-BED OR SOFA
BLANKET
page 116

CUBE STORAGE
SEAT COVER
page 120

BOLSTER CUSHION COVER
page 124

MUG COSY
page 128

TRADITIONAL
CUSHIONS
page 132

getting started

Tools

A hook, scissors and yarn are all the essentials you really need to get started with crochet. Here is a look at those and a number of other items that you may find useful as you progress.

Crochet hooks

Hooks are made in a variety of materials including acrylic, steel, bamboo, wood, bone, plastic, aluminium and silver. Antique silver hooks are rare treasures, so look after them if you have them.

My favourites, and probably the easiest for a beginner to use, are aluminium hooks. They have a flat middle where your thumb goes to stop the hook from spinning around while you work. Your yarns will slide easily over these affordable hooks.

A good hook size to start with would be 4mm (UK8:USG/6), used for most double-knit yarns. The recommended hook size will be stated on the ball bands of most yarns. Enthusiastic crocheters can cheaply buy a complete set of hooks, including a useful range of sizes.

Granny's tip

Buying ergonomic hooks helps if you have painful hands. You could also use rubber bands or pencil grips to give you a better grip on your hooks.

Scissors

A pair of small round-ended scissors is very useful. A good tip is to hang them around your neck on a chain or ribbon. I was always looking for my scissors until I hung them around my neck!

Yarn needle or bodkin

I always weave in the ends with the hook I am using, dealing with them as they happen, but you can also sew off the ends at the completion of a project using a yarn needle or bodkin.

Tape measure or ruler

These are used to check that the tension, or square size, is correct and to work out how many squares you need for a project.

Granny's tip

A toothbrush holder makes a great travel case for your crochet hooks.

Storage

Recycled tins with cute crochet covers are perfect for storing your hooks, scissors and needles – a cheerful way to use up old tins. These also make great storage for pens and pencils.

For yarn storage, you can start with any bag or box, but as your stash grows you will need more and more room. If you are lucky, a designated cupboard is ideal. Plastic trugs are another cheap and cheerful storage idea – perfect if you take your work into the garden. Large, stackable plastic storage boxes are another great solution. You can be very creative with ways to store your yarns, so feel free to use your imagination!

Notebook and pen

I keep extensive notes and file all my ball bands with a small sample of the yarn. It might seem a bit of a hassle to do this but in the long run you will find it extremely useful. Making a note of the yarns, hook size and patterns you use means that you can easily check the details later on when you run out of yarn and need to re-stock. I guarantee that you will never remember what it is called or where you bought it, so keep a note.

Yarns

There are so many fabulous yarns, such as string, fabric, ribbon, cotton, wool, acrylic/wool mixes, merino, alpaca, bamboo, linen, cashmere and silk. Some are easy to crochet with, while others are soft or have fabulous colour ranges.

Yarn weights

Yarns are sold in weights varying from light and lacy to super bulky. However, be aware that even if two yarns are labelled as the same weight they can seem very different.

All yarn weights have a place in the world of today's imaginative crocheter, so be adventurous and experiment with interesting yarns.

Choosing yarns for granny squares

Granny motifs can be made successfully in most yarn types. Changing the hook size to suit the yarn can produce some exciting results – from delicate cotton lacy mats to chunky rugs made from several mixed strands. Never be afraid to experiment with yarn, colour and pattern.

Most beginners start off with acrylic as it is widely available, usually in a good range of lovely colours and very affordable. Ribbon yarns can also be a good first choice if you want a yarn that won't split and can be reasonably priced too.

If the budget will allow, buy a mix of wool and acrylic, usually with up to 70% wool. You will find a good choice of colours and it is perfectly acceptable to mix up brands as long as they are of similar weight. Superwash wool is another good choice for beginners – it won't shrink, will wash and wear well and looks better for longer. The only drawback is if you are allergic to wool.

Pure merino wool is another favourite of mine, particularly the oiled variety. It is slightly finer than the usual DK, but blooms after washing. It can be doubled up for a thick yarn and has a cotton-like appearance. It is easy to work with and can be found in a great range of colours.

If you have an allergy to wool then cotton is a good choice. My advice would be to get a brand with a firm twist, as the hook can sometimes split the yarn, causing much frustration when you are starting out. A cotton and bamboo mix or pure bamboo ribbon is another lovely yarn: beautifully soft and really easy to work with.

When you have become an accomplished crocheter, go for as many exquisite and exciting yarns as you can afford.

Doubling or mixing yarns

Mix two or more of the same or different yarns together and create your own unique blend. This will give a depth to any piece of work, adding great texture – just treat two strands as one.

Tension

A beginner often has difficulty with getting the correct tension. Don't grip the yarn so tightly that your hand and fingers ache. However, not gripping it tightly enough will result in loose and uneven stitches. Practice is the best solution; you could also try watching a friend crochet.

Base-chain runs often work up slightly tighter than the body of the work; try starting with a hook one size larger for the base chain, particularly on a long run of chain stitches, then continue with the correct size. Changing the hook size up or down a size can help to correct your tension when a specific size square is required.

Basic crochet techniques

Beginners can be unsure of how to start off with crochet. These pages will show you the basic techniques. Just remember that crochet is a simple technique of pulling yarn through one or two loops to form a stitch.

Granny's tip

When crochet stitches are worked back and forth (on both sides) you will have a double-sided piece of fabric. However, when worked in the round or from right to left, there is a right and a wrong side. You will learn to recognise the difference.

Holding the hook and yarn

There are two different ways to hold a crochet hook. You will find the one that suits you best as you progress. Here's how I work. Swap the hands if you are left-handed.

1 Hold the hook like a pen, with thumb and index finger on the flat bit of the hook for greatest control, in your right hand.

2 Wrap the yarn around the little finger of your left hand and grip it between the little finger and the ring finger to keep a good tension. The yarn then comes over the back of the hand with the middle finger stretched out a little to enable access to the yarn, and the crochet work is held by the index finger and thumb very close to the working stitch. You will need to move your grip closer every few stitches.

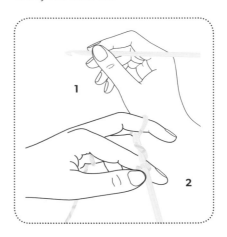

Slip knot (sl k)

The very first thing you will need to start your crochet is a slip knot. Hold the end of the yarn in your left hand, between thumb and index finger, with about an inch (2.5cm) down your palm and the length of yarn over the back of your fingers. Bring the length around your fingers to make a full circle, then pull the length through the circle to make a loop. Holding the loop, pull the short end to form a loose knot, put your hook in the large loop and pull to tighten.

Slip knot (sl k)

Chain stitch (ch)

This is the most basic of all crochet stitches, the first you will learn as a beginner. It is also a very useful and creative stitch.

Chain stitches are used to begin most crochet projects and can be referred to as a starting chain, base chain or a foundation chain. A turning chain is often used between rows and two or three chain stitches are used as a replacement for the first stitch to give the required height.

Chain stitches can be used to create some interesting effects, ranging from decorative loop combinations for edgings (picots) to button loops.

1 Start with a loop on your hook, then bring the yarn around the hook.

2 Pull the yarn through the first loop to form a chain stitch.

3 Repeat through each loop until you have the required number of chain stitches. Front view of chain is shown.

4 Back view of finished chain.

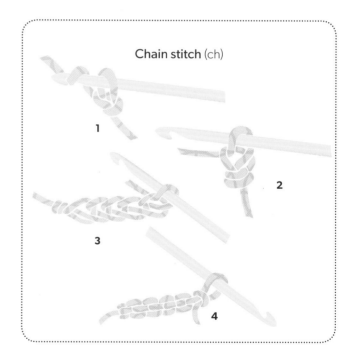

Chain stitch (ch)

Slip stitch (sl st)

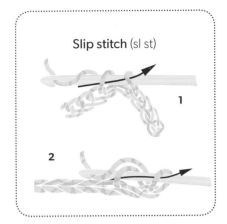

Double crochet (dc)

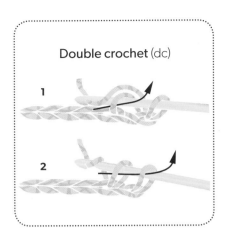

Treble crochet (tr)

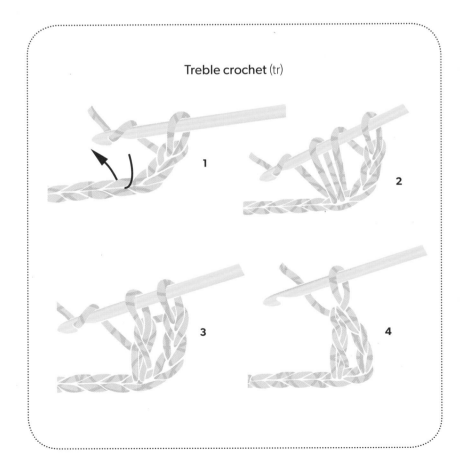

Slip stitch (sl st)

More than just a joining stitch, slip stitch can be used as a decorative stitch or to create a crocheted fabric.

1 With a loop on your hook, push the hook through the base stitch, yarn over hook, pull through the stitch and the loop on the hook.

2 Repeat until you have the required number of stitches.

Double crochet (dc)

A short, firm stitch and one of the easiest stitches to master, double crochet can be made to look quite different depending on which loop you work it through.

1 With a loop on the hook, insert the hook through a base stitch, yarn over hook, pull through the base stitch only. You now have two loops on the hook.

2 Yarn over hook, pull through both loops. You now have a single loop on your hook and the double crochet stitch is complete.

Treble crochet (tr)

Taller than the double crochet and probably the most used of the basic crochet stitches, three trebles worked into a single base stitch form the granny shell.

1 With a loop on your hook, yarn over hook (two loops), push hook through base stitch, yarn over hook then pull through the base stitch.

2 You now have three loops on your hook. Yarn over hook then pull through two loops.

3 You now have two loops on your hook. Yarn over hook then pull through last two loops.

4 You now have a single loop on the hook and the treble crochet stitch is complete.

Double treble (dtr)

This is similar to the treble, incorporating an extra step. Another well-used stitch, it is used to form corners and clusters in this book.

1 With a loop on your hook, wrap the yarn twice around the hook (three loops on the hook).

2 Push the hook through a base stitch, yarn over hook and pull through (four loops on the hook).

3 Yarn over hook and pull through two loops. You now have three loops on the hook.

4 Yarn over hook and pull through two loops. You now have two loops on the hook.

5 Yarn over hook and pull through the last two loops. You now have a single loop on the hook and the double treble stitch is complete.

Cluster stitch

This is a half-made group of three or more treble or double-treble stitches, worked into a single base stitch. They are drawn together on the last pull through. It is a great stitch to form petal shapes and textured stitches.

Treble cluster

1 With a loop on the hook, yarn over hook and push through base stitch. Yarn over hook and pull through (three loops on hook). Yarn over hook and pull through two loops. Hold the two loops on the hook. Repeat the beginning of the treble stitch two or three more times as required, into the same base stitch. (Clusters can be made of three, four or five stitches). Hold the last loop of each stitch on the hook until the group of half-made treble stitches is complete.

2 Yarn over the hook and pull through all the remaining loops, drawing all of the stitches together to make a cluster. Chain one to complete the stitch.

Double treble cluster

1 With a loop on the hook, yarn over hook twice (three loops on hook). Push hook through base stitch, wrap yarn over hook and pull through (four loops on hook). Yarn over hook and pull through two loops (three loops on hook). Yarn over hook, pull through two loops (two loops remaining).

2 Repeat the beginning of the double treble stitch into the same base stitch, holding the last loop of each stitch on the hook, as many times as required.

3 Yarn over hook and pull through all of the remaining loops on the hook to draw all the stitches together to make a cluster. Complete the stitch with a chain stitch.

Shell stitch

A shell is a group of three or more completed treble stitches worked into one base stitch. Shells can be used in an all-over pattern, solid or open. Three trebles worked into the same space or stitch makes the granny shell. Shells can be made with almost all crochet stitches in groups of three or more stitches. Shell stitch can be used to increase and also as a decorative edging stitch.

Open shell stitch

Anchored first round of the open shell stitch used in this book: working from a base round or row of stitches and with a loop on the hook, miss a stitch and do 5 tr sts into the next st, miss a stitch, slip stitch into the next base stitch. Repeat as many times as required to do a round. Multiples of four base-chain stitches are needed for the pattern repeat. Continue working the open shell stitch into the top of each previous shell as follows: start at the top of a shell of the previous round, attaching yarn in the middle stitch. Do 5 tr sts in the same middle stitch, repeat in the top of every shell of the round. Repeat the shell pattern one above the other.

Treble cluster stitch

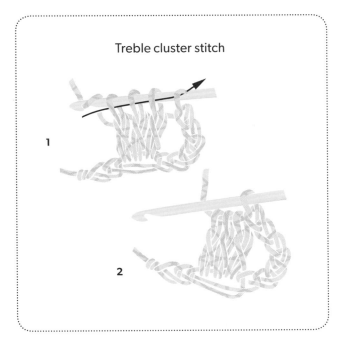

1

2

granny's tip

Clusters and shells can be used in several combinations. They can be mixed with other stitches to form a useful and decorative stitch with many variations.

Shell stitch

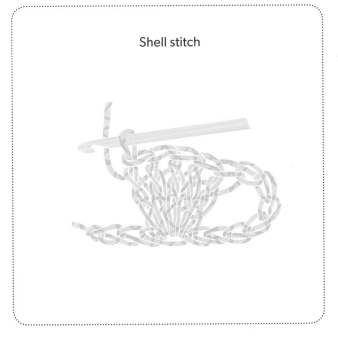

Working in the round

Working in the round is the basis for all granny motifs. First you create a central base ring to work the first round into (using the chain stitch circle or magic circle techniques shown opposite). These can be different sizes depending on the design and whether or not a centre hole is required. Normally the hole will be filled with the first round of stitches that you crochet.

Depending on the stitch to be used in each round, a number of chain stitches are needed to get to the correct height for the stitch. You need one chain for a dc, two for a tr, three for a dtr and so on – each chain equal to each pull through of yarn. Each round is completed with a sl st into the top of the first st in the round.

Sometimes you work each round into the stitch and sometimes into the space between the stitches. This can make a big difference to the look of the design. If you are working in one colour and need to move from the end of one round to the next space, use a sl st into the top of the next few stitches to move across the top of the round to reach the next space, usually only a couple of stitches.

Because the first stitch is usually a set of chain stitches (to achieve the height), the beginning of a round sometimes shows up differently when the project is finished. To help disguise this, start each round at a different point rather than always in the same place. Staggering increase stitches in circular work will also help to hide the beginning and end of a round and keep a perfect circle. If you work increase stitches one on top of the other, a circle will turn into a hexagon quite quickly.

Chain circle

I usually use a four-chain circle that will take 12 or 16 stitches easily. Sometimes the chain circle becomes part of the design and a much larger number of chain stitches is used, forming a hole at the centre of the motif. Make a chain circle as stated in the pattern and join it to make a ring by making a slip stitch into the first chain.

Magic circle

Make a magic circle to give a very tight centre.
1 Make a half-formed slip knot.
2 Do all the first-round stitches into the circle.
3 Pull the end tight after completing one round.

Weaving in ends

I advise you to weave your ends into the back of the stitch at the start and finish of a round and crochet over them. If you leave them until a project is finished there can be a huge number to deal with. On a large, multicoloured bed blanket there could be literally thousands of ends. I always weave in the ends with the hook I am using, never leaving a square unless all the ends have been hidden.

Increasing

Increases are made by doing two stitches into a single stitch of the round below and at regular intervals.

Decreasing

Decrease by missing a stitch or working two stitches together (dc2tog or tr2tog).
1 and 2 Do half a stitch into each of the next two stitches, holding the loops on the hook.
3 Yarn over and pull through both stitches.

Chain circle

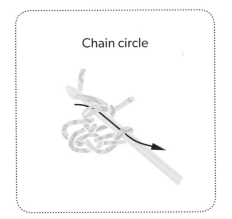

Magic circle

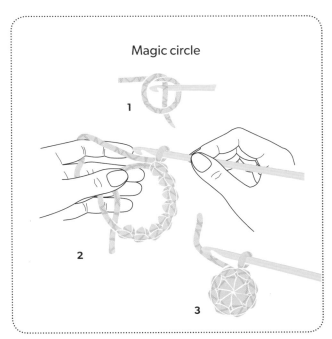

1

2

3

Increasing

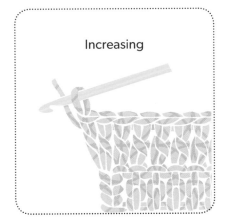

Decreasing

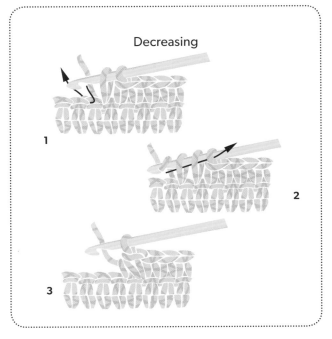

1

2

3

Joining your squares together

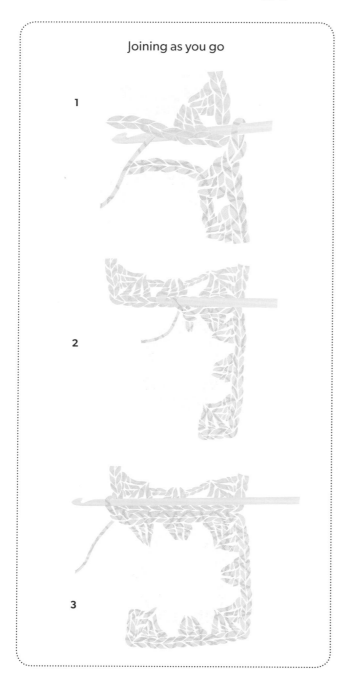

Joining as you go

1

2

3

There are several techniques used for joining your squares together. Always use the same yarn as the project and use a large bodkin-type of needle or a hook of the same size used in the project. I prefer to crochet squares together whenever possible but sometimes sewing your squares together is a good option. If the squares have the same last-round colour, you match the corresponding stitches and stitch them using one of the methods described. If your squares are all different colours, crocheting them together is a far better method.

Joining as you go

This is a simple method of passing the hook through the matching space or stitch of a second square while crocheting the last round. Sometimes with great effect (cable-looking stitch) you can 'join as you go' using every stitch instead of using just the matched spaces to join squares/hexagons together. You can use this method for joining circles, but great care and few joining stitches need to be used to prevent distortion of the circle.

1 Complete the first square. Work a second square up to the last round. You will use the final row to join the two squares. Join the yarn in the corner of the second square. Work the starting chain stitches and two tr sts. Ch 1, sl st to the corresponding chain-one space in the corner of the first square, ch 1. Return to the second square. 3 tr sts to complete corner.

2 Sl st into the corresponding space in the first square, pull yarn through hook. 3 tr sts in second square.

3 Repeat step 2 to the end of the row. In the corner, 3 tr sts, ch 1, sl st into corner of first square, ch 1, 3 tr sts. Complete the round on the second square.

Sewing up

Over stitch or whip stitch

Put two squares together one on top of the other, with right sides facing. Then over stitch, as shown, through the back loops only. This will give a neat ridge on the right side of your project.

Double crochet seams

Place two squares wrong sides together and, matching stitch for stitch, make a dc stitch through both edges of the two squares. This will give a decorative line of stitches if a contrast yarn colour has been used.

Mattress stitch

Matching corresponding stitches are worked back and forth from one edge stitch to the other, pulling the yarn tight after doing three or four stitches. The stitches should disappear inside the work, almost like adding another stitch between the squares.

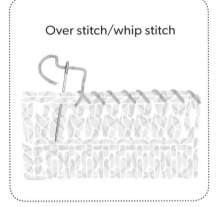

Over stitch/whip stitch

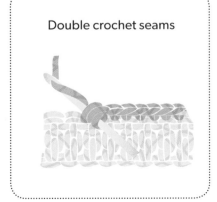

Double crochet seams

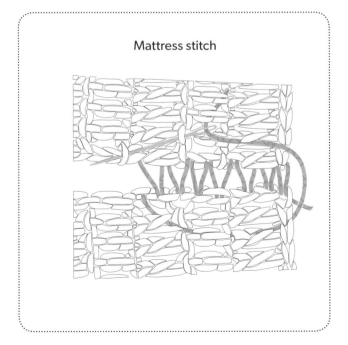

Mattress stitch

Care instructions

Washing instructions are usually found on yarn ball bands, so follow them. If you have mixed different yarns together you will need to take extra care. I always launder with a gentle wash on an 86°F (30°C) setting just in case I have used a pure wool that could felt or shrink. Spin and dry flat, gently pulling the work into shape. Very occasionally I use a tumble drier but *only* on a cool setting.

Granny's tip

Three-dimensional projects can be blocked with household items of the right shape and size, sprayed with water and allowed to dry; you can use small saucepans or balloons for hats or bags.

Blocking your crochet

Blocking will give a finished and professional look to your work. It will shape and set a project, removing wobbles, waves and any distortions. You can dry block or wet block – always following the care instructions on ball bands.

Dry blocking: Lay your dry project out and pin (always use rust-proof pins) into shape on a wet towel, padded board or clean protected carpet and leave to dry.

Wet blocking: Lay your wet project out and pin (always use rust-proof pins) into shape. Spray or lightly steam and then leave to dry.

DO NOT steam man-made yarns, such as acrylic, or hairy yarns, such as mohair or angora. If in doubt, do not block. Hours of work can be destroyed in seconds. I often wait until something needs washing before blocking it.

Problem solving

If your granny shapes look wobbly and uneven
You may have too many stitches for the circumference.

If your granny shapes are curling or cupping
You may not have enough stitches for the circumference.

If you miss a stitch or make a mistake
Unless it is an essential or very visible stitch, don't worry about it. No one will ever find it in a big project, but on a small project it is better to unpick and redo it.

If you run out of yarn a stitch or two from the end of a round
If you just run out by a couple of stitches you can undo a few stitches and then redo them, tightening the tension a little. By doing this, you can often gain enough yarn to do those last couple of stitches.

If you are not in the right place to start the next round
Use slip stitch to move across the top of a previous round to reach the starting space.

If you have problems keeping your yarn clean and tangle-free
Use zip-lock bags for each ball of yarn or use wet-wipes containers with a hole in the top – this will keep your yarn clean and stop it tangling.

If a square or hexagon looks uneven
Check the stitch count – each side of a square or hexagon should have the same number of stitches. Otherwise it may be that your tension is not even.

If your work feels too tight or stiff
A looser tension is needed, so go up a hook size. Do the opposite if the work feels loose and floppy. Find the right hook for the yarn to get the right feel for your work.

If your circles are frilly
Try the '12, 24, 36' rule. Start with a first round of 12 tr sts, second round is 24 tr sts, third round is 36 tr sts. An increase of 12 stitches in each round spread evenly should give you a flat circle in any yarn.

Basic granny shapes

The tradition of making granny shapes comes from humble origins. Once a crochet technique for making patches of fabric from leftover yarns, this thrifty idea has evolved into a creative hobby. Granny squares made up of three or four rounds can be joined together to make a larger project, or kept going to create a giant shape.

Granny square

The granny square is worked from the centre on a base ring of chain stitches and made up of rounds of granny shells (usually three trebles) along each side with chain-stitch corners.

Four-round granny square

Using colour A, ch 4, sl st to form a ring.

Round 1: Using colour A, ch 2 (counts as 1 tr), 2 tr, ch 2, *3 tr, ch 2; repeat from * 2 more times, sl st to complete round (4 sides/4 corners).

Round 2: Using colour B, ch 2 (counts as 1 tr), (2 tr, ch 2, 3 tr) in corner space, *(3 tr, ch 2, 3 tr) in corner space; repeat from * 2 more times, sl st to complete round, weave in ends (2 groups of 3 tr).

Round 3: Using colour C, ch 2 (counts as 1 tr), (2 tr, ch 2, 3 tr) in corner space, 3 tr in side space, *(3 tr, ch 2, 3 tr) in corner space, 3 tr in side space; repeat from * 2 more times, sl st to complete round, weave in ends (3 groups of 3 tr).

Round 4: Using colour D, ch 2 (counts as 1 tr), (2 tr, ch 2, 3 tr) in corner space, 3 tr in 2 side spaces, *(3 tr, ch 2, 3 tr) in corner space, 3 tr in 2 side spaces; repeat from * 2 more times, sl st to complete round, weave in ends (4 groups of 3 tr).

Granny's tip

A three-chain corner will give a squarer, sharper corner and a bigger hole. A one- or two-chain corner will give a rounded corner and a tighter, smaller hole.

Granny circle

There are a number of variations on the granny circle motif. This particular combination will produce a flat granny circle.

Four-round granny circle

Using colour A, ch 4, sl st to form a ring.

Round 1: Using colour A, ch 3 (counts as 1 tr and ch space), *1 tr, ch 1; repeat from * 4 more times, sl st to complete round (6 spokes).

Round 2: Using colour B, ch 2 (counts as 1 tr), 1 tr, (ch 1, 2 tr, ch 1) in first space, *(2 tr, ch 1, 2 tr, ch 1) in next space; repeat from * in each space, sl st to complete round (12 groups of 2 tr plus ch).

Round 3: Using colour C, ch 2 (counts as 1 tr), 2 tr in first space, *3 tr in next space; repeat from * in each space, sl st to complete round (12 groups of 3 tr).

Round 4: Using colour D, ch 2 (counts as 1 tr), 2 tr, ch 1 in first space, *3 tr, ch 1 in next space; repeat from * in each space, sl st to complete round (12 groups of 3 tr plus ch).

Granny hexagon

These attractive six-sided shapes are easily joined into fabulous and decorative projects, each hexagon shape fitting exactly into the next in a staggered pattern.

Four-round granny hexagon

Using colour A, ch 6, sl st to form a ring.

Round 1: Using colour A, ch 2 (counts as 1 tr), 2 tr, ch 1, *3 tr, ch 1; repeat from * 4 more times, sl st to complete round (6 groups of 3 tr and ch 1).

Round 2: Using colour B, ch 2 (counts as 1 tr), (1 tr, ch 2, 2 tr) in same space, *(2 tr, ch 2, 2 tr) in next space; repeat from * in each space, sl st to complete round (12 groups of 2 tr).

Round 3: Using colour C, ch 2 (counts as 1 tr), (1 tr, ch 2, 2 tr) in corner space, 2 tr in side space, *(2 tr, ch 2, 2 tr) in corner space, 2 tr in side space; repeat from * 4 more times, sl st to complete round (18 groups of 2 tr).

Round 4: Using colour D, ch 2 (counts as 1 tr), 2 tr, 2 ch, 3 tr in corner space, 3 tr in side spaces, repeat 5 more times, sl st to complete round (24 groups of 2 tr).

Colour, design and inspiration

Our sense of colour and design is personal and emotional, and can change over time. Colour and design are also determined by trends that change over the decades.

Choosing colour combinations

Colour is a personal thing with many individual associations. I still get it wrong sometimes, even after 40-plus years of study. My motto is, if in doubt use them all – a rainbow always looks good, doesn't it?

If you are struggling to get started, choose lots of shades of a favourite colour. Use some dark and some light to give depth, and then use every shade in between. Join your squares together with cream, white or black – each of these neutrals will pull everything together. Some very random granny squares can be made to look fabulous and quite on-trend when joined together with a neutral colour,

something that makes all those beautiful colours zing. Add a border using a combination of all the colours or black and white – these always make for an interesting frame to a blanket or throw.

Use punched squares, circles and flowers to create a blanket on paper before you commit to expensive yarn buying. See pages 52–3 for a selection of granny-shape designs for you to copy and colour – a great way to try before you buy.

Get inspired

Inspiration can come from many places – a colourful picture or flowery mug, your garden, the room you want to put your blanket or cushion in, a favourite colourful dress, wallpaper patterns and magazine images. Interiors and gardening magazines are good sources for colour inspiration. Study the great colourists of today; Kaffe Fassett and Tricia Guild are two of my favourites. Nature is also always a good source of inspiration.

Experiment with different colour combinations of yarns then make notes on anything you love. Just by changing the yarn colour or the hook size you can change the look of the simplest of squares and create a wonderful new design. Keep all of your experiments; maybe when you have enough you could join them together and make a really beautiful sampler blanket.

Sample designs

Use these drawings
of granny-square designs
for your own colour
and design experiments.
Photocopy, colour,
cut and arrange them
into combinations to your
liking – duplicating,
mixing and matching
to your heart's content.

the projects

Circular Stool Covers

These colourful cotton stool covers are easy to make, easy to fit and easy to wash – perfect for the complete beginner to tackle. A striking accessory for any room, they can be easily adjusted to fit any size of stool.

Finished size

Each stool cover measures 12in (30cm) in diameter. To fit a 12in (30cm)-diameter stool top. Add extra rounds for a bigger stool top or subtract rounds for a smaller one.

You will need

Stool cover version one

- Approx. ¾–1oz (20–30g) each of 8 colours of cotton DK yarn
- 4mm (UK8:USG/6) crochet hook

Stool cover version two

- Approx. ¾–1oz (20–30g) each of 7 colours of cotton DK yarn
- 4mm (UK8:USG/6) crochet hook

Tension

Two 3 dtr clusters measure approx. 1¼in (3cm) wide

Pattern notes

Each round is in a different colour; refer to the photograph for colour changes or be creative with your own colour choices.

Stool cover version one

Ch 6, sl st to form a ring.

Round 1: Ch 2 (counts as 1 tr), 15 tr into circle, 1 sl st to complete round (16 sts).

Round 2: Ch 2 (counts as 1 tr), 1 tr into same st, *ch 2, miss a stitch, 2 tr into next st; repeat from * 7 times, ch 2, sl st to complete round (16 sts).

Round 3: Attach yarn to ch space, ch 3 (counts as 1 dtr), 5 dtr in same space, 6 dtr in each ch 2 space, sl st to complete round (48 sts, 8 groups).

Round 4: Attach yarn in the middle of a 6 dtr group, ch 2 (counts as 1 tr), 2 tr in same st, ch 1, miss 2 sts, *3 tr, ch 1, miss 2 sts; repeat from * to end of round, sl st to complete round (16 groups of 4 sts).

Round 5: Ch 2 (counts as 1 tr), 1 tr in each stitch, sl st to complete round (64 sts).

Round 6: Ch 1 (counts as 1 dc), 1 dc in every stitch, sl st to complete round (64 sts).

Round 7: Ch 3 (counts as 1 dtr), work 2 dtr cluster in same st, *ch 2, miss 1 st, 3 dtr cluster; repeat from * to end of round, ch 2, sl st to complete round (32 clusters).

Round 8: Attach yarn to ch space, ch 2 (counts as 1 tr), 2 tr in same space, *ch 1, 3 tr in next space; repeat from * to end of round, ch 1, sl st to complete round (32 groups).

Round 9: Ch 2 (counts as 1 tr), 1 tr in each st, sl st to complete round (128 sts).

Round 10: Ch 1 (counts as 1 dc), 1 dc in each st, sl st to complete round (128 sts).

Round 11: Ch 2 (counts as 1 htr), 1 htr in each st, sl st to complete round (128 sts).

Round 12: Ch 2 (counts as 1 tr), 1 tr in each st, sl st to complete round (128 sts).

Round 13: Ch 2 (counts as 1 tr), 1 tr in each st, sl st to complete round (128 sts).

Round 14: Ch 2 (counts as 1 tr), 1 tr in each st, sl st to complete round (128 sts).

Add more rounds here for a bigger cover

Round 15: Ch 2 (counts as 1 tr), 1 tr in next 2 sts, *tr2tog, 1 tr in next 3 sts; repeat from * to end of round, sl st to complete round.

Round 16: Ch 1 (counts as 1 dc), 1 dc in every st, sl st to complete round. Keep the tension tight for this round.

Granny's tip

A tighter tension for the last round will make the cover fit closely around the seat; if your tension is loose, use a smaller hook for the last couple of rounds.

Stool cover version two

This stool has a different style of centre and uses different stitch combinations.

Ch 4, sl st to form a ring.

Round 1: Ch 2 (counts as 1 tr), 11 tr into circle, sl st to complete round (12 sts).

Round 2: Ch 3 (counts as 1 dtr), 2 dtr in same st, then 3 dtr in each st to end of round, sl st to complete round (36 sts).

Round 3: Ch 2 (counts as 1 tr), 2 tr in same st, ch 1, miss 2 sts, *3 tr, ch 1, miss 2 sts; repeat from * to end of round, sl st to complete round (48 sts).

Round 4: Ch 1 (counts as 1 dc), 1 dc in every st, sl st to complete round (48 sts).

Round 5: Ch 3 (counts as 1 dtr), work 2 dtr cluster in same st, *ch 2, miss 1 st, 3 dtr cluster; repeat from * to end of round, ch 2, sl st to complete round (24 clusters).

Round 6: Attach yarn to ch space, ch 2 (counts as 1 tr), 2 tr in same space, *ch 1, 3 tr in next space; repeat from * to end of round, ch 1, sl st to complete round (24 granny shells, 96 sts).

Round 7: Ch 2 (counts as 1 tr), 1 tr in each st to end of round, sl st to complete round (96 sts).

Round 8: Ch 2 (counts as 1 tr), work 2 tr cluster in same st, *ch 1, miss 1 st, 3 tr cluster; repeat from * to end of round, ch 1, sl st to complete round (48 clusters).

Round 9: Ch 2 (counts as 1 tr), 2 tr in same space, then 3 tr in each space to end of round, sl st to complete round (48 granny shells).

Round 10: Ch 3 (counts as 1 dc and ch 2), *1 dc in space between shells, ch 2; repeat from * to end of round, sl st to complete round (48 ch loops).

Round 11: Ch 2 (counts as 1 tr), 2 tr in same ch loop, then 3 tr in each ch loop to end of round, sl st to complete round (144 sts).

Round 12: Ch 4 (counts as 1 dc and ch 3), *1 dc in space between shells, ch 3; repeat from * to end of round, sl st to complete round (48 ch loops).

Round 13: Ch 2 (counts as 1 tr), 2 tr in same ch loop, then 3 tr in each ch loop to end of round, sl st to complete round (144 sts).

Round 14: Ch 2 (counts as 1 tr), 1 tr in each st to end of round, sl st to complete round (144 sts).

Round 15: Ch 2 (counts as 1 tr), 1 tr in each st to end of round, sl st to complete round (144 sts).

Add more rounds here for a bigger cover

Round 16: Ch 2 (counts as 1 tr), 1 tr in next 2 sts, *tr2tog, 1 tr in next 3 sts; repeat from * to end of round, sl st to complete round (116 sts – there are not quite enough sts to make 29 decreases).

Round 17: Ch 1 (counts as 1 dc), 1 dc in every st, sl st to complete round. Keep the tension tight for this last round (116 sts).

Version one

Version two

Tablet Computer Case

Carry your new tablet computer around with style while protecting it from some surface everyday wear and tear. This case is colourful, practical and makes a great gift, too.

Finished size

10 x 8in (25 x 20cm)
To fit a 9½ x 7½in (24 x 19cm) tablet computer

You will need

- Approx. 3–3½oz (90–100g) in total of small quantities of any pure wool DK in a variety of colours
- 4mm (UK8:USG/6) crochet hook
- 12in (30cm) zip-fastener
- Yarn needle
- 6 feet (2m) of matching yarn for sewing up

Tension

Each granny square measures 2 x 2in (5 x 5cm)

One-colour granny squares

(make 40)

Ch 4, sl st to form a ring.
Round 1: Ch 2 (counts as 1 tr), 2 tr, *ch 2, 3 tr; repeat from * 3 times, ch 2, sl st into second ch st to complete round (4 sides/4 corners).
Round 2: Sl st in first ch space, ch 2 (counts as 1 tr), (2 tr, ch 2, 3 tr) in same ch space, (3 tr, ch 2, 3 tr) in each following ch space, sl st to complete round, weave in ends (4 sides/4 corners).

Making up

You can sew the squares together, but join as you go (see page 44) is a better method when joining lots of different squares together. Join the squares so you have two pieces that are 4 x 5 squares each.

Side band

A band of 3 rows makes the case wide enough to add a piece of foam to the inside to protect your computer tablet.
Round 1: Colour A. 1 dc in every stitch, sl st to complete round, weave in ends (144 sts).
Round 2: Colour B. 1 dc in every stitch, sl st to complete round, weave in ends (144 sts).
Round 3: Colour A. 1 dc in every stitch, sl st to complete round, weave in ends (144 sts).

Finishing

Stitch the two pieces together, matching the stitches as you go and leaving a 12in (30cm) opening for the zip-fastener – stitching one square down along one long side and one square down along the opposite end is just the right size. Hand-stitch the zip-fastener in place.

granny's tip

To make up one side of your tablet case in two-colour granny squares, as I have done (see photo opposite), simply change the colour for the second round.

Notebook Cover

Turn your dull shopping lists into something
special with this essential little notebook cover.
Made up of 24 two-round granny squares,
it would make a fun gift for friends or family.

Finished size

11½ x 7½in (29 x 19cm)
To fit a 10½ x 6¾ (27 x 17cm) spiral notebook

You will need

- Approx. 2oz (60g) in total of scraps of DK wool in lots of colours (A–B in pattern)
- 4mm (UK8:USG/6) crochet hook
- Large button (approx. 1⅛in [3cm] diameter)

Tension

Each granny square measures 2in (5cm) square

Pattern notes

Each round is in a different colour; refer to the photograph for colour changes or be creative with your own colour choices.

Two-round granny squares

(make 24, all different)

Ch 4, sl st to form a ring.
Round 1: Using colour A, ch 2 (counts as 1 tr), 2 tr, *ch 2, 3 tr; repeat from * 3 times, ch 2, sl st into second ch st to complete round, cut and weave in ends (4 sides/ 4 corners).
Round 2: Join colour B in a ch space, ch 2 (counts as 1 tr), (2 tr, ch 2, 3 tr) in same ch space, (3 tr, ch 2, 3 tr) in each following ch space, sl st to complete round, cut and weave in ends (4 sides/4 corners).

Making up

You can sew the squares together, but joining as you go (see page 44) is a better method when joining lots of different colours together. Assemble the squares so you have a piece that is 4 x 6 squares.

Edge stitch main body of cover before attaching the securing ends as follows: work 1 dc in every stitch around the four sides of the cover, sl st to complete round, sew in ends (160 sts).

Securing ends

(make 2)

Work a flat piece back and forth in the chosen edging colour as follows. Ch 33.
Row 1: 1 tr into 3rd ch from hook, 1 tr into each ch to end.
Rows 2–5: Ch 2 to turn, 1 tr in each st.

Finishing

Place the end pieces, one each end, wrong sides together with the short end of main cover. Match the stitches as you go and work the two pieces as one. Work 1 dc in every stitch to attach the ends to the main body, sl st to complete round and sew in ends.

Make a loop of ch sts big enough for your chosen button in the middle of one of the short sides and sew the button to the middle of the other short side; sew in ends securely.

Star Coasters

A six-petal flower inside a star makes an ideal shape
for a handy coaster. This is a fabulously simple beginner's project
that is quick and easy to achieve – so you can make coasters by the
dozen in an array of sumptuous colourways.

Finished size

Approx. 4¼in (11cm) diameter

You will need

- Approx. 1¾oz (50g) in total of 3 colours of DK cotton yarn will make 8 coasters
- 4mm (UK8:USG/6) crochet hook

Tension

Not crucial to project

Pattern notes

Each round is in a different colour; refer to the photograph for colour changes or be creative with your own colour choices.

Coaster

Ch 4, sl st to form a ring.
Round 1: Ch 2 (counts as 1 tr), 11 tr into circle, sl st to complete round, cut and weave in ends (12 sts).
Round 2: Ch 3 (counts as 1 dtr), 1 dtr in same st, 2 dtr in next st, *ch 3, 2 dtr in next 2 sts; repeat from * 5 times, ch 3, sl st to complete round, cut and weave in ends (6 petals).

Round 3: Join yarn in ch 3 space, ch 2 (counts as 1 tr), (2 tr, ch 3, 3 tr) in first space, *dc in middle st of 'petal' grouping, (3 tr, ch 3, 3 tr) in next space; repeat from * 5 times, 1 dc in middle st of last petal grouping, sl st to complete round, cut and weave in ends (6-pointed star).

Granny's tip

All the rounds are in a different colour, but they could be made in a single colourway for a quicker project. Alternatively, simply join the stars together to create the building blocks for many other exciting projects.

Felted Flower Bag

Here is a quick and exciting project for the beginner using multicoloured randomly dyed wool yarn. This funky granny-flower, hexagon-design bag has a felted finish, so make sure you use felting wool to make it.

Finished size

17 x 12in (43 x 30cm)

You will need

- Approx. 10½oz (300g) in total of felting wool in 3 different colours (A–C in pattern/3½oz [100g] in each colour)
- 9mm (UK00:USM/13) crochet hook
- Yarn needle

Tension

Not crucial to project

Pattern notes

Motif uses a dtr cluster stitch, which is explained on page 40.

Hexagon motif
(make 13 using three colours interchangeably)

Using A, ch 4 and sl st to form a ring.

Round 1: Using A, ch 2 (counts as 1 tr), 11 tr into the circle, sl st to complete round, cut and weave in ends (12 sts).

Round 2: Using B, attach yarn to any stitch, to make petals do clusters of 3 dtr (ch 3 as first dtr) with ch 2 between each cluster, sl st to complete round, cut and weave in ends (12 clusters).

Round 3: Using C, attach yarn in any space, ch 2 (counts as 1 tr), 2 tr in same space, 3 tr in next space, ch 2, *3 tr in next space, 3 tr in next space, ch 2; repeat from * 4 more times, sl st to complete round, cut and weave in ends (6 sides/6 corners).

Making up

Lay two hexagons side by side and over stitch (see page 45) with one of the colours; join all 13 hexagons together as in the diagram.

Side bands
(make two)

Attach chosen yarn at point X in diagram, work four rows back and forth of 16 dc into the two side hexagons, sew in ends; repeat on the other side (two side bands).

Handle (make two)

Make a longer strap (increase the number of ch sts) if you want to turn it into a shoulder bag.

Round 1: Attach chosen yarn at point Y in diagram, 36 dc along top edge, ch 20, sl st to complete round.

Round 2: Ch 2 (counts as 1 dc), 1 dc in the next 11 sts, miss a stitch, 1 dc in the next 10 sts, miss a st, 1 dc in the next 12 sts, 1 dc in each of the ch 20 handle, sl st to complete round.

Round 3: Ch 2 (counts as 1 dc), 1 dc in the next 11 sts, miss a stitch, 1 dc in the next 8 sts, miss a st, 32 dc in the next 32 sts, sl st to complete round.

Round 4: Ch 2 (counts as 1 dc), 1 dc in the next 11 sts, miss a st, 1 dc in the next 6 sts, miss a st, 32 dc in 32 sts, sl st to complete round. Weave in ends.

Repeat handle on the other side.

Felting

Always follow the instructions on the ball band of the felting wool you are using. Place the bag in the washing machine with a pair of jeans to add to the agitation. Set the washing machine to 104°F (40°C). If more felting is needed after one cycle, reset and continue until you get the desired size.

Felted flower bag construction diagram

Using the diagram: The easiest way to see how the construction of the bag comes together is to photocopy and cut out the diagram and fold along the lines shown. You will then have a clear three-dimensional model of the bag.

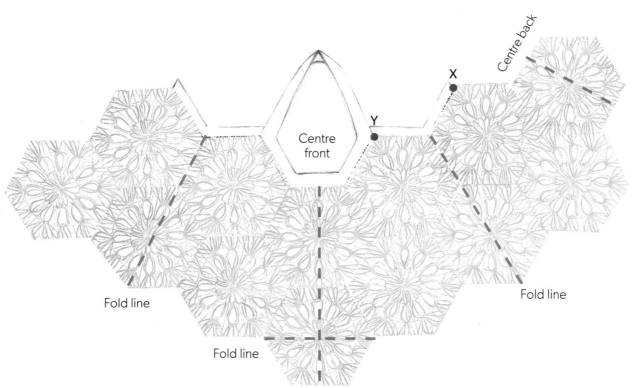

Centre back

X

Y

Centre front

Fold line

Fold line

Fold line

String Shopping Bag

If you are new to crochet it is great fun to
experiment with as many different yarns as possible.
String is a perfect choice for this fun vintage bag
made up of 13 individual granny squares.

Finished size

18 x 17in (46 x 43cm)

You will need

- Approx. 10 small balls of soft cotton parcel string (574yd [525m] each). Or, 21oz (600g) in total weight of string.
- 9mm (UK00:USH-N/13) crochet hook
- 10mm (UK000:USN-P/15) crochet hook

Tension

Not crucial to project

Three-round granny squares
(make 13)

Using the 10mm hook, ch 4, sl st to form a ring.

Round 1: Ch 2 (counts as 1 tr), 2 tr, *ch 2, 3 tr; repeat from * 3 times, ch 2, sl st into second ch st to complete round (4 sides/4 corners).

Round 2: Sl st to first ch space, ch 2 (counts as 1 tr), (2 tr, ch 2, 3 tr) in same ch space, (3 tr, ch 2, 3 tr) in each following ch space.

Round 3: Sl st to corner ch space, ch 2 (counts as 1 tr), (2 tr, ch 2, 3 tr) in corner space, *3 tr in side space, (3 tr, ch 2, 3 tr) in corner space; repeat from * 3 times, 3 tr in side space, sl st to complete round.

Making up

For this project you will need to perfect the join as you go method (see page 44). The open look to the bag would make it difficult to get a good finish stitching the squares together. Join the squares as shown in the diagram.

Side bands
(make two)

Change to 9mm hook.

Row 1: Attach string at point X on diagram, 1 dc in each stitch of sides of two squares (23 sts).

Row 2: Ch 2, turn and work back along row of dc, 1 dc in next 11 sts, miss a stitch to make a 'v', 1 dc in next 11 sts.

Row 3: Ch 2, turn and work back along row of dc, 1 dc in next 10 sts, miss a stitch, 1 dc in next 11 sts, finish off leaving a couple of inches (about 5cm) of string.

Repeat on the other side of the bag.

Straps
(make two)

Use 9mm hook.

Round 1: Attach string at point Y in diagram, 1 dc in next 31 sts, ch 40 (strap), sl st to complete round.

Round 2: Ch 2 (counts as 1 dc), 1 dc in next 14 sts, miss a st, forming a 'v', 1 dc in next 15 sts, 1 dc in each of the 40 ch sts, sl st to complete round.

Round 3: Ch 2 (counts as 1 dc), 1 dc in next 13 sts, miss a st, 1 dc in next 15 sts, dc in next 40 sts of strap, sl st to complete the round.

Repeat for the second strap.

Weave in any ends.

String shopping bag construction diagram

Using the diagram: The easiest way to see how the construction of the bag comes together is to photocopy and cut out the diagram and fold along the lines shown. You will then have a clear three-dimensional model of the bag.

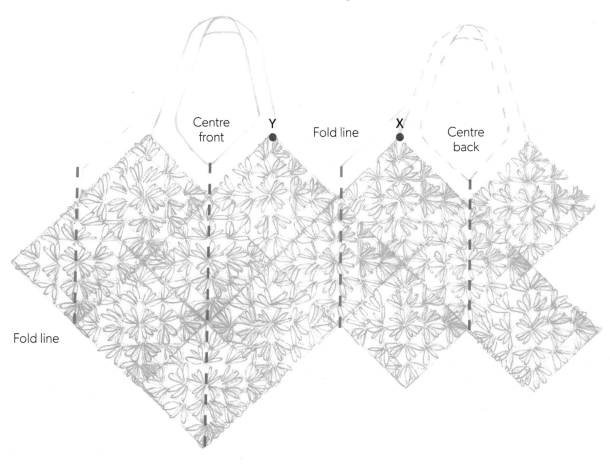

Garden Seat Cover

Easy-to-make two-colour 'spot' granny squares in 12 summer
colours make a cheerful seat cover that will brighten up
any beach or garden party. The cover is easy to remove and wash
and it can be easily adapted for larger or smaller chairs.

Finished size

45½x 20in (116 x 52cm)
To fit a garden seat of the above dimensions. Add extra rows of squares as required to fit different-sized chairs using the individual granny-square measurements below as a guide.

You will need

- Approx. 1oz (30g) of 12 different colours of merino DK
- Approx. 1oz (30g) of 12 different colours of acrylic DK (same colours as merino)
- Approx. 22oz (625g) of cream merino DK as background yarn (used double)
- 5mm (UK6:USH/8) crochet hook
- Yarn needle

Tension

Each square measures approx. 5in (13cm) square

Pattern notes

The cover is made using a strand of merino and a strand of acrylic yarn worked together as one strand.

Granny's tip

If you like, you can vary the circles by making each round a different colour.

Circle motif

(make 3 each in 12 colours plus 8 extra, total 44)

Using chosen colour, ch 4, sl st to form a ring.
Round 1: Ch 2 (counts as 1 tr), 11 tr into circle, sl st to complete round (12 tr).
Round 2: Ch 4 (counts as 1 tr and ch 2), *1 tr in next space, ch 2; repeat from * until you have 12 spokes, sl st into the ch 4 loop (12 spokes).
Round 3: Ch 2 (counts as 1 tr), 2 tr into first ch space, 3 tr in each space around, sl st to complete round (36 sts).
Round 4: Using cream colour, attach yarn in line with a spoke, ch 4, *1 dc into 3rd tr, ch 4; repeat from * 11 times, sl st into first ch loop (12 loops).
Round 5: Ch 2 (counts as 1 tr), (2 tr, ch 2, 3 tr) in first ch loop, *3 dc in next loop, 3 dc in next loop, (3 tr, ch 2, 3 tr) in next loop; repeat from * 2 more times, 3 dc in next loop, 3 dc in next loop, sl st into first ch 2 to

complete round, cut and weave in ends (4 sides/4 corners).
Round 6: Ch 2 (counts as 1 tr), 1 tr in next 2 sts, *(1 tr, ch 2, 1 tr) in corner space, 1 tr in next 12 sts; repeat from * 3 times, (1 tr, ch 2, 1 tr) in last corner, 1 tr in next 9 sts, sl st to complete round (4 sides of 14 tr).

Making up

Main seat cover: Over stitch the squares together matching the stitches (see page 45); stitch four squares together in nine rows.
Securing ends (make two): Over stitch four squares together, matching the stitches. After stitching them together, add two rows of dc along one long side of each of these securing ends. With wrong side of securing ends to wrong side of cover, work two rounds of dc around the whole cover, matching motifs and stitches as you go; sl st to complete round and weave in ends.

Securing ties: Ch 30, attach to the edge of the 4th row of motifs with a dc, ch 30, pull yarn through to finish, trim off leaving ends of about 1in (2.5cm). Tie to back of garden chair after fitting ends over the top and bottom of the chair.

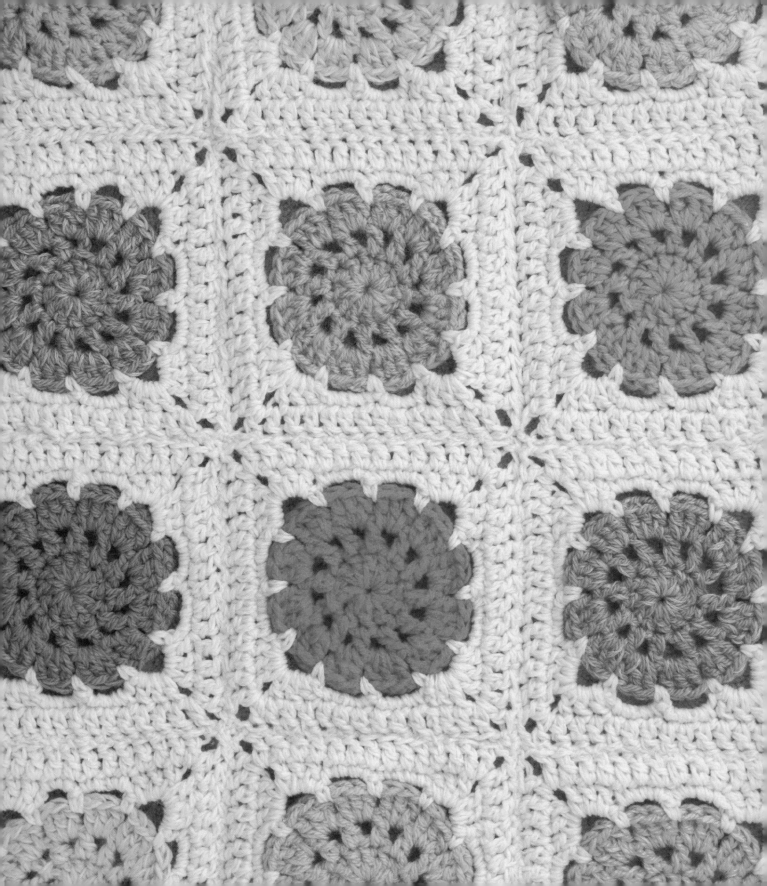

Hexagon Daisy Bath Mat

Making this soft and cosy bath mat is a great way to use up small leftover bits of yarn and will make a quirky addition to your bathroom. Every daisy motif is made in three different colours.

Finished size

29 x 19in (74 x 48cm)

You will need

- Approx. 5¾oz (160g) in total of small quantities of merino DK in lots of colours (A–C in pattern)
- Approx. 5¾oz (160g) in total of small quantities of acrylic DK in lots of colours (same as merino)
- 5mm (UK6: USH/8) crochet hook
- Yarn needle

Tension

Not crucial to project

Pattern notes

Motif uses a dtr cluster stitch; see page 40 for instructions. One strand of merino and one strand of acrylic are worked together. Each round is in a different colour; refer to the photograph for colour changes or you can be creative with your own colour choices.

Granny's tip

You can make a simpler version of the bath mat by using just one colour, or make all of the hexagons in the same three colours.

Hexagon motif

(make 29 in as many colours as you want)

Using colour A, ch 4 and sl st to form a ring.

Round 1: Using A, ch 2 (counts as 1 tr), 11 tr into the circle, sl st to complete round, cut and weave in ends (12 sts).

Round 2: Using B, attach yarn to any stitch, to make petals do clusters of 3 dtr (ch 3 as first dtr) with ch 2 between each cluster, sl st to complete round, cut and weave in ends (12 clusters).

Round 3: Using C, attach yarn in any space, ch 2 (counts as 1 tr), 2 tr in same space, *(3 tr, ch 2, 3 tr) in next space, 3 tr in next space; repeat from * 5 times, (3 tr, ch 2, 3 tr) in next space, sl st to complete the round, cut and weave in ends (6 sides/ 6 corners).

Making up

Lay two hexagons right sides together and over stitch (see page 45) using one of the colours; join all 29 hexagons together. Alternatively, use the join as you go method (see page 44).

Hexagon Bed Pillow

This pretty pillow is a gorgeous accessory
for dressing your bed in a homely and inviting style.
It can also be used as a comfortable back support
for leisurely breakfasts in bed.

Finished size
25 x 16in (64 x 41cm)
To fit a 25 x 16in (64 x 41cm)
pillow pad

You will need
- Approx. ½–¾oz (15–20g) each of merino DK in lots of colours (A–C in pattern)
- Approx. ½–¾oz (15–20g) each of acrylic DK in lots of colours (same as merino)
- Approx. 9oz (260g) cream merino DK for background
- Approx. 9oz (260g) cream acrylic DK for background
- 5mm (UK6:USH/8) crochet hook
- 5 buttons (approx. ⅞in [2.25cm] diameter)

Tension
Each side of a hexagon measures 5in (13cm)

Pattern notes
Each of the motifs is made using a strand of merino and a strand of acrylic yarn worked as one strand to give a slightly flecked appearance. Rounds 1–3 are each in a different colour. Round 4 makes the background colour. Refer to the photograph for colour changes or you can be creative with your own colour choices.

Hexagon motif
(make 40 using random colours)
Using A, ch 4, sl st to form a ring.

Round 1: Using A, ch 2 (counts as 1 tr), 11 tr into circle, sl st to complete round, cut and weave in ends (12 sts).

Round 2: Using B, attach yarn in any stitch, ch 3 (counts as 1 dtr), 2 dtr in same st, 3 dtr in each st to end of round, sl st to complete round, cut and weave in ends (36 sts).

Round 3: Using C, attach yarn between a 3 dtr group, ch 2 (counts as 1 tr), 2 tr in same st, *ch 1, 3 tr in space between 3 dtr group; repeat from * to end of round, ch 1, sl st to complete round, cut and weave in ends (36 sts).

Round 4: Using background colour, attach yarn in any ch 1 space, ch 2 (counts as 1 tr), (2 tr, ch 2, 3 tr) in first space, *3 tr in next space, (3 tr, ch 2, 3 tr) in next space; repeat from * 5 times, 3 tr in next space, sl st to complete round, cut and weave in ends (6 corners/6 sides).

Making up
Stitch hexagons together as shown on the diagram or use the join as you go method, see page 44. Fold the piece and stitch together as shown in diagram leaving three hexagon points open on one side; stitch on five buttons to close the opening. Natural holes in the crochet work form the buttonholes.

Hexagon bed pillow construction diagram

Using the diagram: The easiest way to see how the construction of the
pillow comes together is to photocopy and cut out the diagram and
fold along the lines shown. You will then have a clear three-dimensional
model of the pillow.

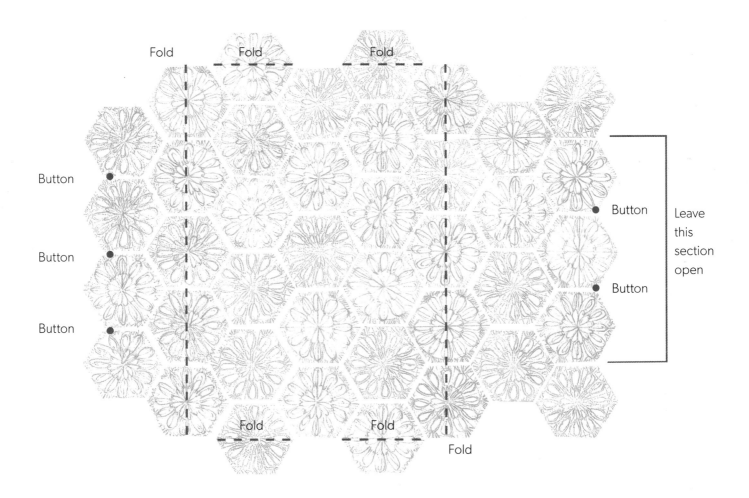

Camping Blanket

This attractive vintage-look blanket is perfect for wrapping
up in during those chilly evenings around the campfire.
The one-colour motifs can be as bold or as subtle as you like.

Finished size

Approx. 36 x 36in (92 x 92cm)

You will need

- Approx. ⅓oz (10g) per colour of 36 colours of merino DK
- Approx. ⅓oz (10g) per colour of 36 colours of acrylic DK (same colours as merino)
- Approx. 2½oz (75g) cream cashmere/merino blend DK
- Approx. 2½oz (75g) cream merino DK
- Approx. 1oz (30g) black cashmere/merino blend DK
- Approx. 1oz (30g) black merino DK
- 5mm (UK6:USH/8) crochet hook
- Yarn needle

Tension

Not crucial to project

Pattern notes

Each of the coloured motifs is made using a strand of merino and a strand of acrylic yarn worked as one strand to give a slightly flecked appearance. The cream background and the black accent are made by using the cashmere/merino blend and merino worked together as one strand.

Wheel in a square motif

(make 49 in a variety of colours)

Ch 4, sl st to form a ring.

Round 1: Ch 2 (counts as 1 tr), 11 tr into circle, sl st to complete round (12 tr).

Round 2: Ch 4 (counts as 1 tr and ch 2), *1 tr in next space, ch 2; repeat from * until you have 12 spokes, sl st into the ch 4 loop (12 spokes).

Round 3: Ch 2 (counts as 1 tr), 2 tr into first ch space, then 3 tr in each space, sl st to complete round (36 sts).

Round 4: Ch 4, *1 dc into 3rd tr, ch 4; repeat from * 11 times, sl st into first ch 4 (12 loops).

Round 5: Ch 2 (counts as 1 tr), (2 tr, ch 2, 3 tr) in first loop, *3 dc in next loop, 3 dc in next loop, (3 tr, ch 2, 3 tr) in next loop; repeat from * 2 more times, 3 dc in next loop, 3 dc in next loop, sl st into first ch 2 to complete round, cut and weave in ends (4 sides/4 corners).

Round 6: Using cream, start in a corner space, ch 4 (counts as 1 tr and ch 2), 1 tr in corner space, *1 tr in next 12 sts, (1 tr, ch 2, 1 tr) in corner space; repeat from * 2 more times, 1 tr in next 12 sts, sl st to 2nd ch of first ch 4 to complete round (4 sides/4 corners).

Making up

Decide on the colour placement of the squares and, with right sides together, over stitch (see page 45) from the back. Sew in all ends.

Border

Round 1: Using cream, start in a corner, (1 tr, ch 2, 1 tr) in the corner space, 1 tr in every stitch; repeat for all 4 sides, sl st to complete round.

Round 2: Change to black, (2 dc, ch 2, 2 dc) in the corner space, 1 dc in every stitch; repeat for all 4 sides, sl st to complete round.

Round 3: Change to cream, (1 dc, ch 2, 1 dc) in the corner space, 1 dc in every stitch; repeat for all 4 sides, sl st to complete round.

Round 4: Change to black, 2 dc in the corner space, 1 dc in every stitch; repeat for all 4 sides, sl st to complete round.

granny's tip

As a lighter and slightly smaller alternative, this blanket could be made with one strand of DK yarn and a 4mm crochet hook.

Hexagon Blanket

This five-round hexagon-motif blanket has a simple but pretty fleur-de-lys-style edge. Its delicate detailing makes it a great blanket for all ages, from new baby to granny or grandad.

Finished size

Blanket assembled in large hexagon shape: 41in (104cm) across widest point, 23in (58cm) along one side of hexagon.

You will need

- Approx. 10oz (270g) superwash merino DK in small quantities of as many colours as you want (A–B in pattern)
- Approx. 10oz (270g) superwash merino DK in cream/natural for background
- 4mm (UK8:USG/6) crochet hook

Tension

Not crucial to project

Pattern notes

Rounds 1–3 are made in two colours. Rounds 4–5 make the background colour. Refer to the photograph for colour changes or be creative with your own colour choices.

Circle-centred hexagons
(make 91)

Using colour A, ch 4, sl st to form a ring.

Round 1: Using A, ch 2 (counts as 1 tr), 11 tr into the circle, sl st to complete round, cut and weave in ends (12 sts).

Round 2: Using B, attach yarn in any space, ch 4 (counts as 1 tr and ch 2), *1 tr in next st, ch 2, repeat from * until you have 12 spokes, sl st into the ch 4 (12 spokes).

Round 3: Ch 2 (counts as 1 tr), 2 tr into first ch space, then 3 tr in each space, sl st to complete round, cut and weave in ends (36 sts).

Round 4: Using natural colour, attach yarn in line with a spoke, ch 4, *1 dc into 3rd tr, ch 4, repeat from * 11 times, sl st into first ch 4 loop (12 loops).

Round 5: Sl st into next ch loop, ch 2 (counts as 1 tr), 2 tr in same space, *(3 tr, ch 2, 3 tr) in next space, 3 tr in next space, repeat from * 5 times, (3 tr, ch 2, 3 tr) in next space, sl st to complete round, cut and weave in ends (6 sides).

Making up

Sew the individual hexagons together into a large hexagon shape, starting with a central motif and then adding another five circular rows around it. You can also use the join as you go technique (see page 44).

Finishing –
fleur-de-lys edge

Attach natural-coloured yarn at an outer point, *ch 4, sl st into same space, ch 6, sl st into same space, ch 4, sl st into same space (fleur-de-lys), 1 dc in 9 tr sts of the hexagon side, miss 2 sts at dip, 1 dc in 9 tr sts of hexagon side, sl st into next point, repeat from * all around the blanket making a fleur de lys at each point and missing 2 sts at each dip; sl st to complete, weave in ends.

Flower Light Shade

A fun and simple way to add a subtle touch of granny chic to your interiors. This is another great project for using up leftover bits of yarn; it can easily be adjusted to fit other sizes of light shade.

Finished size

16in (41cm) diameter,
8in (20cm) deep.
To fit a circular light shade of the above dimensions. Adjust the number of squares you make to fit any straight-sided light shade using the individual granny-square measurements below to calculate how many are needed.

You will need

- Approx. 5oz (130g) in total of three colours of merino DK or cotton DK (A–C in pattern)
- Approx. 2½oz (75g) cream merino DK or cotton DK as background yarn
- 4mm (UK8:USG/6) crochet hook
- Yarn needle

Tension

Each granny square measures 4½in (12cm) square

Pattern notes

Rounds 1–3 are each in a different colour. Rounds 4–5 make the background colour. Refer to the photograph for colour changes or you can be creative with your own colour choices.

Granny-square flower motif
(make 22)

Using A, ch 4, sl st to form a ring.
Round 1: Ch 2 (counts as 1 tr), 11 tr into circle, sl st to complete round, cut and weave in ends (12 tr).
Round 2: Using B, ch 3 (counts as 1 dtr), 2 dtr cluster in same st, *ch 2, 3 dtr cluster in next st; repeat from * to end of round, ch 2, sl st to complete round, cut and weave in ends (12 dtr clusters).
Round 3: Using C, attach yarn in any space, ch 2 (counts as 1 tr), 2 tr in same space, *ch 1, 3 tr in next space; repeat from * 11 times, ch 1, sl st to complete round, cut and weave in ends (36 sts).
Round 4: Using cream colour, attach yarn in any space, ch 2 (counts as 1 tr), (2 tr, ch 2, 3 tr) in same space, *ch 1, 3 dc in next space, ch 1, 3 dc in next space, ch 1, (3 tr, ch 2, 3 tr) in

next space; repeat from * 3 times, ch 1, 3 dc in next space, ch 1, 3 dc in next space, ch 1, sl st to complete round (4 sides/4 corners).
Round 5: Ch 2 (counts as 1 tr), 1 tr in next 2 sts, *(1 tr, ch 2, 1 tr) in corner space, 1 tr in next 13 sts; repeat from * 2 more times, (1 tr, ch 2, 1 tr) in corner space, 1 tr in next 10 sts, sl st to complete round, cut and weave in ends (15 tr on each side 2 ch corner).

Making up

Sew two rows of 11 granny squares together then join the short edges to make a circle.

Finishing

Round 1: Using cream colour, attach yarn in any st at top edge of shade, ch 1 (counts as 1 dc), 1 dc in every st, sl st to complete round (187 sts).
Round 2: Ch 1 (counts as 1 dc), 1 dc in every st, sl st to complete round, cut and weave in ends.
Repeat around the bottom edge.
Fit cover onto the light shade.

Lace Light Shade

This wider version of the granny-shell pattern produces a really pretty stitch that you can make into all sorts of lacy decorations. This light shade, which can easily be adapted for any size of straight-sided shade, will cast a lovely diffused light on your room.

Finished size

Approx. 26in (66cm) circumference and 9in (23cm) high.
To fit a light shade of the above dimensions. See pattern notes for how to adjust sizing.

You will need

- Approx. 2¾oz (80g) of cream or white 4-ply cotton yarn or two strands of a finer cotton yarn
- 4mm (UK8:USG/6) crochet hook

Tension

Each five-shell repeat measures 6in (15cm)

Pattern notes

One cream and one white strand are held together to create a slight texture. This shade took 23 shells per round and each shell needs four base stitches, so it can be easily adjusted to fit any size shade, so long as you have multiples of 4 stitches.

Light shade

Make a chain of 92 sts, sl st to the first ch to form a ring, being very careful not to twist the chain.

Round 1: 1 dc in each st as a base on which to work the shell pattern (92 sts).

Round 2: *Miss a st, 5 tr into the next st, miss a st, sl st into the next st; repeat from * until you have 23 shells, sl st to complete round.

Round 3: Sl st in the next 3 sts to reach the centre of first shell, ch 2 (counts as 1 tr), 4 tr in the same st, *5 tr in the 3rd tr of the next shell; repeat from * until all 23 shells are finished, sl st into second ch of first ch 2 to complete round.
Repeat round 3, 14 more times (16 shell rounds).
Cut and weave in ends.
Place around light shade.

Granny's tip

You could choose colours to match your décor. To make a funkier light shade, you could use a different colour for each round, make the shade with ribbon yarns or try using a mixture of interesting yarns.

Lace Jar Cover and Coasters

The wider granny-shell pattern also makes a useful cover for a jar.
The cover is a smaller version of the light shade (see page 104), with
the addition of a coaster or two for the bottom of the jar and other
items. Use the cover to make a pretty vase out of an empty jar, or to
decorate a tea-light holder.

Finished size

Jar cover: approx. 10in (25cm) circumference and 3½in (9cm) tall

Coaster: approx. 4½in (11cm) diameter

To fit a jar or tea-light holder of the above dimensions. See pattern notes for how to adjust sizing.

You will need

- Approx. 1½oz (40g) of cream and white 4-ply cotton yarn or two strands of a finer cotton yarn
- 4mm (UK8:USG/6) crochet hook

Tension

Each five-shell repeat measures 6in (15cm)

Pattern notes

One cream and one white strand are held together to create a slight texture. The shell stitch requires four base-chain stitches per shell so size adjustments can be made to suit any size jar or tea-light holder.

Jar cover

Ch 4, sl st to form a ring.

Round 1: Ch 2 (counts as 1 tr), 11 tr into circle, sl st to complete round (12 sts).

Round 2: Ch 2 (counts as 1 tr), 1 tr in same st, 2 tr in each st, sl st to complete round (24 sts).

Round 3: Ch 2 (counts as 1 tr), 1 tr in same st, 1 tr in next st, *2 tr in next st, 1 tr in next st; repeat from * around, sl st to complete round (36 sts).

Round 4: Ch 2 (counts as 1 tr) go back 2 sts and anchor with a sl st, 4 tr into original st, *miss a st, sl st in next st, miss a st, 5 tr in next st, repeat from * 8 times, sl st into second ch of first ch 2 (9 shells).

Round 5: Sl st in the next 3 sts to reach the centre of first shell, ch 2 (counts as 1 tr), 4 tr in the same st, *5 tr in the 3rd tr of the next shell; repeat from * until all 9 shells are finished, sl st into second ch of first ch 2 to complete round.

Repeat round 5 as many times as your chosen vessel requires.

Cut and weave in ends. Slip the cover onto your vessel, add a tea light and place it on the coaster.

Coaster for jar

Ch 4, sl st to form a ring.

Round 1: Ch 2 (counts as 1 tr), 11 tr into circle, sl st to complete round (12 sts).

Round 2: Ch 2 (counts as 1 tr), 2 tr in each stitch, sl st to complete round (24 sts).

Round 3: Ch 2 (counts as 1 tr), 1 tr in same st, 1 tr in next st, *2 tr in next st, 1 tr in next st; repeat from * around, sl st to complete round (36 sts).

Round 4: Ch 2 (counts as 1 tr), 1 tr in same st, 1 tr in next 2 sts, *2 tr in next st, 1 tr in next 2 sts; repeat from * around, sl st to complete round (48 sts).

Round 5: *Miss a stitch, 5 tr in the next stitch, miss a st, sl st into the next stitch; repeat from * until you have 12 shells, sl st into first st to complete round.

Cut and weave in ends.

Hexagon Mini Cushion

Place a cushion inside this cover to rest your head
upon for reading in bed, or use it as a pouch to store
your pyjamas. This cover is made up of eight five-round
flower hexagons and has a neat button fastening.

Finished size

14in (35cm) from point to point of assembled hexagon shape

You will need

- Approx. 2oz (60g) in total of several colours of merino DK (A–D in pattern)
- Approx. 2oz (60g) in total of several colours of cashmere/ merino blend DK (same colours as merino)
- Approx. 1½oz (40g) cream or white merino DK (used double)
- 5mm (UK6:USH/8) crochet hook
- Star-shaped button (approx. ¾in [2cm] from point to point)

Tension

Each side of a hexagon measures 3¾in (9.5cm)

Pattern notes

The cushion is made using a strand of merino and a strand of cashmere/ merino blend held together as one strand. The motif uses tr and dtr cluster stitches; see pages 40-41. Rounds 1–4 are each in a different colour. Round 5 makes the background colour. Refer to the photograph for colour changes or be creative with your own colour choices.

Flower hexagon motif
(make eight)

Using A, ch 4, sl st to form a ring.

Round 1: Ch 2 (counts as 1 tr), 11 tr into circle, sl st to complete round, cut and weave in ends (12 tr).

Round 2: Using B, ch 2 (counts as 1 tr), 2 tr cluster in same st, *ch 2, 3 tr cluster in next st; repeat from * to end of round, ch 2, sl st to complete round, cut and weave in ends (12 tr clusters).

Round 3: Using C, attach yarn in a chain space, ch 3 (counts as 1 dtr), 2 dtr cluster in same ch space, *ch 3, 3 dtr cluster in next ch space; repeat from * to end of round, ch 3, sl st to complete round, cut and weave in ends (12 dtr clusters).

Round 4: Using D, attach yarn in any space, ch 2 (counts as 1 tr), (2 tr, ch 2, 3 tr) in first space, *3 tr in next space,

(3 tr, ch 2, 3 tr) in next space; repeat from * 5 times, 3 tr in next space, sl st to complete round, cut and weave in ends (6 sides).

Round 5: Using background colour, attach yarn in a corner ch space, ch 2 (counts as 1 tr), *1 tr in next 9 sts, (1 tr, 2 ch, 1 tr) in corner space; repeat from * 5 times, 1 tr in next 9 sts, 1 tr in first corner space, ch 2, sl st to complete round, cut and weave in ends (6 sides of 11 tr with ch 2 corners).

Making up

Sew the pieces together and fold as shown in the diagram. Leave two sides of the middle hexagon open on one side for inserting the pillow or pyjamas. Stitch on the button. The buttonhole will be formed from natural holes in the crochet work.

Hexagon mini cushion construction diagram

Using the diagram: The easiest way to see how the construction of the cushion comes together is to photocopy and cut out the diagram and fold along the lines shown. You will then have a clear three-dimensional model of the cushion.

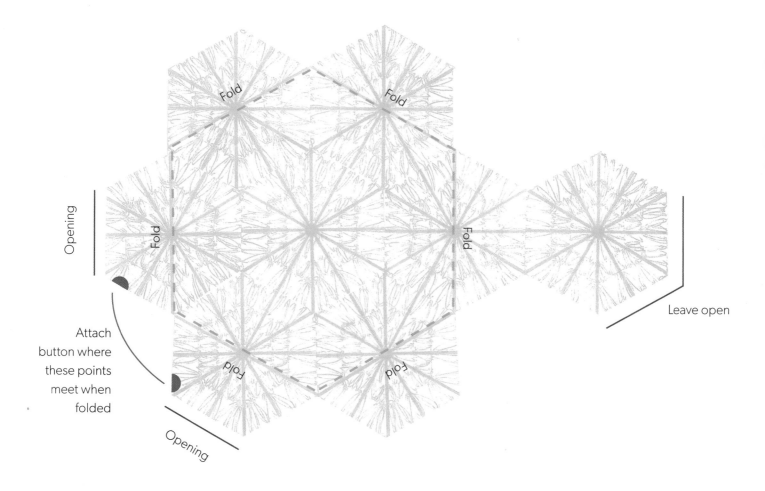

Fold

Fold

Fold

Fold

Fold

Fold

Fold

Opening

Opening

Leave open

Attach button where these points meet when folded

Double-Bed or Sofa Blanket

Making a bed or sofa throw is a big project, one to be picked up and put down often. But by making a few squares at a time you will eventually create a fabulous family heirloom. Using lots of different colours yields a vintage feel.

Finished size

58in (147cm) square
To fit a standard double bed

You will need

- 20 x 1¾oz (50g) balls of pure wool or merino DK in lots of colours (A–C in pattern)
- Approx. 10½oz (300g) cream/white pure wool or merino DK for background
- Approx. 1¾oz (50g) black pure wool or merino DK for the border
- 4mm (UK8:USG/6) crochet hook

Tension

Not crucial to project

Pattern notes

Every round in each square is a different colour. Aim to make every square a different colour combination, but you will find some colours become favourites and repeats can happen. Refer to the photograph for colour changes or you can be creative with your own colour choices.

Circle motif

Using colour A, ch 4, sl st to form a ring.

Round 1: Ch 2 (counts as 1 tr), 11 tr into circle, sl st to complete round, cut and weave in ends (12 sts).

Round 2: Using colour B, attach yarn to any space, ch 4 (counts as 1 tr and ch 2), *1 tr in next st, ch 2; repeat from * until you have 12 spokes, sl st into the 2nd ch of first ch 4 to complete round, cut and weave in ends (12 spokes).

Round 3: Using colour C, attach yarn to any space, ch 3 (counts as 1 dtr), 2 dtr into first ch space, *ch 3, 3 dtr in next ch space; repeat to end of round, ch 3, sl st to complete round, cut and weave in ends (36 cluster sts).

Making up

If using the join as you go method, (see page 44), wait to work round 4 until you have all the middles finished. Decide on the colour placement and complete round 4 with join as you go in rows of 14 squares.

If sewing the squares together, proceed to round 4 and finish all squares, then decide on colour placement and sew the squares together in rows of 14 squares.

Round 4: Using cream/white, attach yarn to any chain space, ch 3 (counts as 1 dtr), (2 dtr, ch 3, 3 dtr) in same space, *ch 1, 3 tr, ch 1, 3 tr, ch 1, (3 dtr, ch 3, 3 dtr); repeat from * 3 times, ch 1, 3 tr, ch 1, 3 tr, ch 1, sl st to complete round, cut and weave in ends (4 corners/4 sides).

Finishing border

Work 3 rounds of granny shells and a firming dc last round as follows:

Round 1: Attach cream/white at a corner, ch 2 (counts as 1 tr), (2 tr, ch 3, 3 tr) in corner space, 3 tr in each side space, *(3 tr, ch 3, 3 tr) in corner space, 3 tr in each side space; repeat from * 2 more times, sl st to complete round (70 granny shells on each side).

Round 2: Attach black at a corner and repeat round 1 (71 granny shells on each side).

Round 3: Attach cream/white at corner and repeat round 1 (72 granny shells on each side).

Round 4: Using cream/white, work 1 dc in every stitch and 3 dc at each corner.

Sew or weave in any remaining ends.

Granny's tip

A blanket of 14 by 14 squares is large enough to cover the top of a double bed. If you want a bigger blanket, add more rows of squares before working the border.

Cube Storage Seat Cover

A couple of changes to the first two rounds of a basic granny square makes a very pretty daisy granny. It's not only great for this cube storage-seat cover, but also makes a wonderful alternative granny square for many other projects.

Finished size

12 x 12in (30 x 30cm)
To fit a cube seat of the above
dimensions. Add extra rows of
squares as required to fit different
sized cube seats using the individual
granny-square measurements below
as a guide.

You will need

- Approx. 1¼oz (35g) pale yellow
  cotton DK for centres (A)
- Approx. 2½oz (70g) white or
  cream cotton DK for the daisy (B)
- Approx. 7oz (200g) in total of
  small quantities of cotton DK in
  lots of colours (C)
- Approx. 8oz (230g) green cotton
  DK as background colour (D)
- 4mm (UK8:USG/6) crochet hook

Tension

Each granny square measures
4 x 4in (10 x 10cm)

Daisy motif

(make 45)

Ch 4 and sl st to form a circle.
Round 1: Using A, ch 4 (counts as
1 tr and ch 2), *1 tr in next st, ch 2;
repeat from * 7 times, sl st into the
2nd ch of first ch 4 to complete
round, cut and weave in ends
(8 spokes).
Round 2: Using B, attach yarn to
any ch space, ch 2 (counts as 1 tr),
2 tr in same space, ch 1, *3 tr in next
space, ch 1, repeat from * 7 times,
sl st to complete the round, cut and
weave in ends (8 granny shells).
Round 3: Using C, attach yarn to
any ch space, ch 2 (counts as 1 tr),
(2 tr, ch 2, 3 tr) in the same space,
3 tr in the next space, *(3 tr, ch 2,
3 tr) in next space, 3 tr in next space,
repeat from * 2 more times, sl st to
complete round (12 granny shells,
4 corners/4 sides).
Round 4: Using D, attach yarn to
corner space, ch 2 (counts as 1 tr),
(2 tr, ch 2, 3 tr) in the corner space,
3 tr in the next two side spaces,
*(3 tr, ch 2, 3 tr) in the next space,
3 tr in the next two side spaces;
repeat from * 2 more times, sl st to
complete round (16 granny shells,
4 corners/4 sides).
Round 5: Ch 1 (counts as 1 dc),
1 dc in every st, working 3 dc in the
corners, sl st to complete round (12
sts each side, 3 sts at corners).

Making up

With right sides together and
matching stitches, over stitch (see
page 45) the squares together in five
groups of nine. Then stitch the cube
top and four sides together. Sew in
all remaining ends.

Finishing

To finish the open bottom of the
cube cover and firm up the edge,
work a round of dc, one stitch in
each previous stitch.

Bolster Cushion Cover

By turning a granny square on end like a diamond, you
can create a bolster cushion cover with an all-over design.
Working with two strands of similar coloured yarns
held together creates a unique and slightly tweedy look.

Finished size

21in (54cm) circumference and 17in (43cm) length. To fit bolster cushion 24in (61cm) circumference and 18in (45cm) length.

You will need

- Approx. 4¼oz (120g) in total of several shades of wool/acrylic blend or superwash wool DK (A–B in pattern)
- Approx. 4¼oz (120g) in total of similar colours of fine merino DK (A–B in pattern)
- Approx. 2oz (60g) yellow wool/acrylic blend or superwash wool DK for background
- Approx. 2oz (60g) of similar shade of fine merino DK
- 5mm (UK6:USH/8) crochet hook
- 3 buttons (approx. ¾in [2cm] diameter)

Tension

Each square measures 3½ x 3½in (9 x 9cm)

Pattern notes

Motif uses 2 dtr clusters; see page 40. Each of the coloured motifs, including the yellow background, is made using a strand of merino and a strand of wool/acrylic blend or superwash wool worked as one strand.

Motif
(make 36, changing colour for each round)

Using A, ch 4 and sl st to form a circle.

Round 1: Ch 2 (counts as 1 tr), 11 tr into the circle, sl st to complete round, cut and weave in ends (12 sts).

Round 2: Using B, attach yarn in any space, ch 3 (counts as 1 dtr), 2 dtr cluster in same st, *ch 2, 3 dtr cluster; repeat from * to end of round, ch 2, sl st to complete round, cut and weave in ends (12 cluster sts).

Round 3: Change to background colour, attach yarn in any corner space, ch 2 (counts as 1 tr), (2 tr, ch 3, 3 tr) in same space to make corner, 2 dc in next 2 spaces, *(3 tr, ch 3, 3 tr) in next space, 2 dc in next 2 spaces; repeat from * 2 more times, sl st to complete round (4 corners/ 4 sides).

Making up

Sew the squares together as shown on the main diagram opposite, and then make a tube and join it together lengthways. At the non-opening end of the bolster, sew the square sides together (see small diagram A).

To form the opening end, sew the opposite sides together leaving an opening from one side of the bolster to the other (see small diagram B).

Opening
(at one end only)

Attach the background yarn at one side and work a round of dc with loops as follows:

1 dc in next 24 sts (down one side of the opening), work along other side of opening with *1 dc in the next 6 sts, ch 5, return to the same stitch; repeat from * 2 more times, finish with 1 dc in last 6 sts, sl st to complete opening, cut and weave in ends. Sew on three buttons opposite loops.

Bolster cushion cover construction diagram

Using the diagram: The easiest way to see how the construction of the cushion cover comes together is to photocopy and cut out the diagram and fold along the lines shown. You will then have a clear three-dimensional model of the cushion cover.

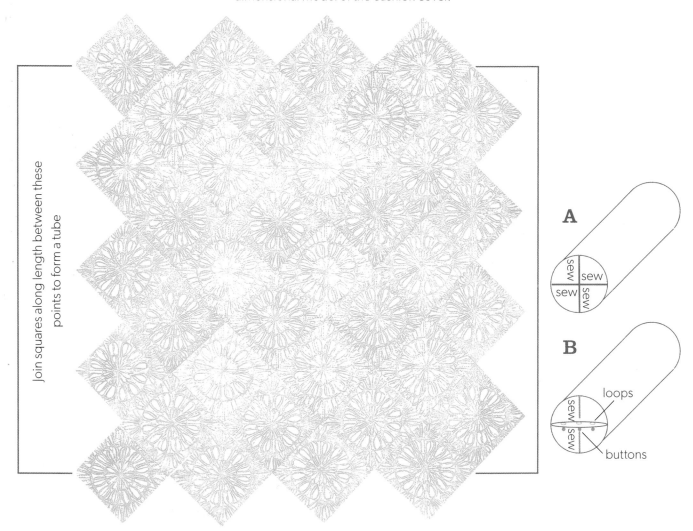

Join squares along length between these points to form a tube

A

sew sew
sew sew

B

sew
sew

loops

buttons

Mug Cosy

Keep your coffee warm on a cold winter's day
with this decorative open shell stitch in a rainbow of
colours. Make it in two sizes just by changing the thickness
of cotton and the hook size, or make a set in one colour
to coordinate with your kitchen.

Finished size

5 x 6in (13 x 15cm)
To fit mug measuring approximately 4in (10cm) in diameter and 4in (10cm) tall

You will need

Cream cosy
- Approx. 1oz (30g) cotton 4-ply
- 4mm (UK8:USG/6) crochet hook

Rainbow cosy
- Approx. 1oz (30g) in total of small quantities of cotton DK in different colours
- 5mm (UK6:USH/8) crochet hook
- Button

Tension

Not crucial to project

Pattern notes

The pattern is the same for both versions; the only difference is the yarn and hook size and the number of rounds needed for your mug. Multiples of four base stitches are needed to do a shell stitch.
If making the rainbow cosy, use a different colour for each round.

Mug cosy

Ch 4, sl st to form a ring.
Round 1: Ch 2 (counts as 1 tr), 11 tr into circle, sl st to complete round (12 sts).
Round 2: Attach yarn in any st, ch 2 (counts as 1 tr), 2 tr in each stitch, sl st to complete round (24 sts).
Round 3: Attach yarn in any st, ch 2 (counts as 1 tr), 1 tr in same st, 1 tr in next st, *2 tr in next st, 1 tr in next st; repeat from * until round complete, sl st to complete round (36 sts).
Shell-stitch sides (rounds of 9 open shells)
Round 4: Ch 2 (counts as 1 tr), go back 2 sts and anchor with a sl st, 4 tr into original st, *miss a st, sl st in next st, miss a st, 5 tr in next st, repeat from * 8 times, sl st into second ch of first ch 2 (9 shells).

Round 5: If making the rainbow cosy, attach yarn to 3rd tr of shell below. If making the one-colour cosy, sl st to centre of first shell. Ch 2 (counts as 1 tr), 4 tr in the same st, *5 tr in the 3rd tr of the next shell; repeat from * until all 9 shells are finished, sl st into second ch of first ch 2 to complete round (9 shells).
Round 6: If making the rainbow cosy, attach yarn to 3rd tr of shell below. If making the one-colour cosy, sl st to centre of first shell. Ch 2 (counts as 1 tr), 4 tr in the same st, *5 tr in the 3rd tr of the next shell; repeat from * until 8 shells completed, the 9th shell is made of 4 tr, and ch 2 as the last tr, sl st back into same stitch.
Repeat round 6 as many times as needed for your mug.
Final round: Repeat round 6, but the last shell is made with 4 tr, and ch 4, sl st into same stitch to make a button loop to go over the top of the mug handle.

Finishing

Weave in all ends. Sew on a button, using the photographs as a guide for placement.